DECODABLE BOOK 2

Orlando   Boston   Dallas   Chicago   San Diego

Visit *The Learning Site!*

www.harcourtschool.com

Requests for permission to make copies of any part of the work should be addressed to School Permissions and Copyrights, Harcourt, Inc., 6277 Sea Harbor Drive, Orlando, Florida 32887-6777. Fax: 407-345-2418.

HARCOURT and the Harcourt Logo are trademarks of Harcourt, Inc., registered in the United States of America and/or other jurisdictions.

Printed in the United States of America

ISBN 0-15-326682-1

14 179 10 09 08 07

Ordering Options
ISBN 0-15-323767-8 (Collection)
ISBN 0-15-326716-X (package of 5)

Contents

Ham? Hat?

by Gail Williams

illustrated by
Chris Van Dusen

Max had a ham.

Jan had a hat.

A ham?

A hat?

Have a ham, Jan.

Have a hat, Max.

Max has the hat!
Jan has the ham!

Tap a Hat

by Mary Hogan

illustrated by Pam Paparone

Dad has a hat.

Tad has a hat.

Dad can pat the hat.

Pat, pat, pat.

Tad can tap the hat.

Tap, tap, tap.

Can you tap a hat?

Ham? Hat?

Word Count: 30

High-Frequency Words

have
the

Decodable Words*

a
had
ham
has
hat
Jan
Max

*Words with /a/*a* appear in **boldface** type.

Tap a Hat

Word Count: 32

High-Frequency Words

the
you

Decodable Words*

a
can
dad
has
hat
pat
Tad
tap

*Words with /a/*a* appear in **boldface** type.